The Software Conductor

*A journey of discovery from software
developer to architect*

Lee Atchison

Published by *Atchison Academy* in the United States of America.

All artwork in this book was created by ChatGPT 5.1 from prompts created by the author.

Identifiers:

979-8-9960196-0-1 (Paperback)
979-8-9960196-2-5 (Hardcover)
979-8-9960196-1-8 (Ebook)

To Beth

My love, my life, my everything

Contents

Part Three
Mentoring and Coaching

Part Four
The Big Picture

Part Five
The Architect Emerges

♪ Prelude ♪

I started writing this book three times before.

The first two times, I wrote what I thought a software architecture book was supposed to be. Chapters with section headings. Frameworks with acronyms. Bulleted lists explaining the difference between a developer and an architect. A book whose value is measured in its hefty page count. The book was complete. I had a publisher ready to pull the trigger and publish it. I even started promoting it on social media.

But I knew something was off. The book was technically correct, and entirely lifeless.

I had been trying to teach architecture the way I once tried to lead it. From the front of the room, with the diagrams.

I called the publisher, canceled the contract. The book wasn't going to go out.

That was three years ago...

♪ ♪ ♪

Here's what I've learned over thirty-some years of doing this work, across companies large and small. The hardest part of becoming a software architect isn't the technical knowledge. The hardest part is learning to see your job differently. To stop measuring your contribution by how much code you write. To stop being the hero who solves every problem. To start asking what others need before telling them what they should do.

That part is hard to teach in bullet points.

So I tried a third time, and what came out was a story.

The story is about three people. Aaron is a developer who wants to become an architect but doesn't quite know how. Anton is an orchestra conductor who teaches him what leadership looks like when you're responsible for what others create rather than what you create yourself. Rachel is the friend who keeps Aaron honest, who reminds him that systems are built by people and that the people are the system.

I've put pieces of every architect I've ever worked with into Aaron. Pieces of every mentor I've ever had into Anton. Pieces of every colleague who saw something in me before I did into Rachel. None of them are real. All of them are real. That's how stories work.

This book is for anyone who's started to feel there's more to this craft than building features. It's for the senior developer wondering whether to take the leap. It's for the new architect who's pretty sure they're doing it wrong. It's for the engineering leader who hires architects and wants to understand what they're actually buying.

Read it as a story. Read it as a song. The lessons will land where they need to.

There's a baton waiting at the end, and someone needs to pick it up.

It might as well be you.

— *Lee*

Part One

The Wakeup Call

Chapter 1

♪ *The First Note* ♪

Aaron slumped into his seat and loosened his tie.

He did *not* want to be there. He'd spent all week buried in sprint meetings and code reviews, and now his friend Rachel had dragged him to some local orchestra concert event.

"You need to get out of your head," she'd said. "There's more to life than debugging code."

The lights dimmed. The murmur of the audience quieted. A figure stepped onto the stage. And with a single flick of his wrist, the conductor brought fifty musicians to life.

Violins, cellos, flutes, trumpets. Everyone was playing different notes, different rhythms, yet somehow forming one coherent sound.

It was beautiful.

Aaron leaned forward. The precision at which the players worked fascinated him.

He watched the conductor's small, sharp gestures:

> a raised eyebrow for the violins
> a subtle nod to the percussion
> a sweeping motion to bring the brass section
> forward

The man didn't make a sound himself. Not one note. Not one word. But it was clear that the music was his creation all the same.

Aaron thought about his own week. It was filled with the chaos of code merges, API changes, and endless "urgent" fixes. Every developer working on their part of the application, each one sure their piece was the most important. And Aaron trying to hold it all together so it wouldn't fall apart into complete disaster.

He smirked. *If only our team had a conductor,* he thought.

Before Aaron could realize it, it was intermission. The lights came up, and Aaron and Rachel stepped into the lobby.

"So," Rachel said, sipping a cup of coffee. "Better than a code review?"

Aaron laughed. "Yeah. Actually... it kind of reminds me of one."

A voice beside him joined in. "I hope that's a compliment."

Aaron turned. Standing next to the snack table was the conductor himself, still in his tuxedo, holding a bottle of water and smiling.

"It is," Aaron said quickly. "I'm a software developer. Watching you up there was amazing. It felt like you were running an engineering team. Everyone's doing something different, but it all fits together. You're like... the architect."

The conductor chuckled. "Architect! Hmm, yes. But without the hard hat."

Aaron chuckled too. "Yeah, a *software* architect. I'm trying to *become* one! An architect, I mean. Not a conductor. Though maybe that's the same thing."

The tuxedoed man tilted his head, studying him with interest. "And what's stopping you?"

Aaron hesitated. "Letting go, I guess. I like building things, writing the code myself. Whenever there is a problem, I'm the one that has to fix it. Nobody else understands what it is that I need to do to fix things.

"But I know architects are supposed to focus on the big picture, not the details."

"Ah." The conductor smiled knowingly. "You're still trying to play the violin while waving the baton."

Aaron blinked, a comical vision of a violinist trying to handle a baton and a bow string at the same time filling his mind. "Yeah...that's exactly what it feels like!"

The conductor extended his hand. "I'm Anton."

"Aaron."

"Well, Aaron," Anton said, "the hardest part about conducting isn't learning the notes. It's learning to trust that others will play them."

Aaron nodded slowly. The words hit deeper than he expected.

Anton continued. "A conductor doesn't tell every musician how to move their fingers. He gives direction: the tempo, balance, and overall mood. And then he steps back. If he tries to control every sound, the entire musical piece falls apart."

Aaron smiled faintly. "Sounds like our application at work. It keeps falling apart."

Anton laughed. "Maybe you need to step back. You might be closer to being a conductor than you think." He reached into his jacket and pulled out a small business card.

"Come to our rehearsal next week," he said. "You'll see what real coordination looks like. Bring your laptop, if you must. But I promise you" The conductor poked a finger knowingly at Aaron, "you'll learn something."

Aaron took the card. "You're serious?"

"Completely."

"And now, if you'll excuse me, I need to get ready for the second act." The conductor disappeared through a side door.

A short time later, the lights blinked in the lobby, it was the signal that the concert was about to continue.

Aaron looked down at the card. *Anton Weiss, Conductor*.

He slipped it into his pocket and smiled. For the first time that week, he felt a little less stuck.

Chapter 2

♪ *The 3 a.m. Pager Call* ♪

Aaron's monitor still glowed from the emergency that had jolted him awake six hours earlier.

The problem was fixed. A simple memory leak in a service nobody remembered owning. Nobody really cared about it for that matter, until it failed. He'd patched it, restarted the system, and messaged the incident channel with *"All clear."*

The problem was fixed. The incident was over. He had saved the day...again.

The adrenaline had drained out of Aaron, leaving only an empty spirit.

Now it was 10:15 a.m. The office smelled like burnt coffee and recycled air. His head buzzed, his eyes dry and heavy. The hum of the air conditioner felt like white noise from another planet.

He stared at the open terminal window on his laptop, not reading it, not even really seeing it.

The cursor blinked, steady and patient, like it could out wait him. It could, he knew it could.

A shadow appeared near him, and then a bump on his desk.

It was Rachel.

"Green tea with ginger," she said, setting the cup beside his keyboard. "You look like death warmed over."

Aaron rubbed his eyes. "Thanks, that's a great line coming from you."

Rachel smiled. She had a designer's knack for aesthetics, even when teasing him about his appearance. It was part of why she was the product designer on his project, and his closest friend.

Aaron continued, "Actually, that sounds better than I feel. I feel like death burned to a crisp in the broiler."

More somberly now, Rachel asked, "You were paged again?"

"Yeah. Three a.m. this time. Database pool exhaustion. I think I aged a year watching the connections stack up."

"Sounds thrilling."

"Oh, absolutely. Nothing like debugging a database connectivity issue at 3 a.m. while the world sleeps peacefully."

Rachel sat on the corner of his desk, sipping from her own mug. "You ever wonder if this is it? If this is what we're supposed to be doing forever?"

He looked up. "What, chasing alerts and half-baked deadlines?"

She shrugged. "You tell me."

Aaron leaned back in his chair, letting out a tired laugh. "Lately, I can't tell if I'm building systems or if they're just building stress."

Rachel studied him for a moment: his slouched shoulders, the darkened circles under his eyes. She'd seen this version of him before. It was his burnout cycle, the one that never showed up in his code reviews but lived behind his quiet sarcasm.

She changed approaches. "So," she said, "how did you enjoy your *big cultural outing* last night?"

Aaron groaned. "You mean the concert you dragged me to?"

"Yes, that one," she said, ignoring his tone.

He sighed. "It was... actually... interesting. The conductor, Anton Weiss, he... I don't know, there was something about how he moved. Everything looked chaotic, but somehow..."

"But somehow..." Aaron scrunched up his face in pained thought, "somehow it wasn't."

"Wasn't what???"

"It wasn't chaotic."

Rachel's eyes lit up. "See? You noticed."

"I'm not sure what I noticed. Just... It's just that the orchestra responded to him. It responded to him like code responding to a perfect commit. Every part synced up. It was so cool."

She smiled. "That's what happens when someone understands the system."

Aaron raised an eyebrow. "You sound like him."

"Oh? He already gave you a lecture?"

"Not exactly. After the show, he asked me if I understood what I saw."

"And you said..." she let the question hang.

Aaron hesitated. "I said he made a hundred people move as one."

Rachel nodded, prompting him to continue.

"He said, 'Nope. *But I listened until they did.*'"

Aaron took a sip of his tea, the warmth cutting through his fatigue. "That line's been stuck in my head ever since."

Rachel watched him quietly. "He invited you to a rehearsal, didn't he?"

"Yeah," Aaron said. "Tonight. But I don't think I'll go. I've got a sprint review tomorrow, and after last night...I'm just too drained."

She cut him off. "You're going."

Aaron frowned. "Rachel!"

"Nope. You're going. You've been restless for months, Aaron. You keep saying you want to 'see the bigger picture.' Well, maybe it's time to actually start *looking*."

He chuckled softly. "You think a conductor's baton is going to fix my career crisis?"

"I think you might learn something if you stop ignoring the world for five minutes."

Aaron smirked. "That's unfair. I work hard at my job. It takes a lot of focus."

"I know," she said, leaning forward with a smile. "That's why you need me as your friend. Sometimes, maybe you need to step back from the code and listen to the orchestra."

For a long moment, the two sat quietly.

Aaron's mind drifted. It drifted to the flicker of the conductor's hands. It drifted to the surge of the violins, the silent language of connection he'd seen on that stage. He felt something in it. Something beyond syntax and sprint cycles. Something he couldn't yet name.

Rachel nudged his arm. "So?"

He sighed, pretending to resist. "Fine. I'll go."

She grinned. "Good. Maybe he'll teach you how not to look like a zombie."

Aaron chuckled. "No promises."

As Rachel stood and walked back to her desk, Aaron glanced again at his terminal. The cursor still blinked. But this time he wasn't intimidated by it. It wasn't taunting him. It was more like a heartbeat.

He closed the laptop. Maybe he'd try and catch a nap this afternoon.

Tonight, he'd go to the rehearsal.

♪ ♪ ♪

LESSON: THE DEVELOPER'S FATIGUE

Great engineers fix what's broken. But great architects learn *why* it keeps breaking.

Aaron's sleepless night wasn't just about a faulty database connection. It was about a system stretched thin because no one was watching the whole. The parallel symbolism to his life was unmistakable.

> *The conductor doesn't stay awake tuning every violin. He listens for imbalance and teaches the players to hear it themselves.*

The big picture is not about control. It's not about understanding everything. It's about understanding how everything works together.

Chapter 3

♪ *The Rehearsal* ♪

That evening, Aaron stood in the back of Benaroya Hall again, only this time, there was no audience.

No chatter. No programs rustling.

Just the hum of fluorescent lights and the faint echo of chairs sliding across the stage.

He almost turned back. He wasn't sure why he'd come. Curiosity, maybe. Or guilt. Rachel's "you're going" was still ringing in his ears.

He tugged at his hoodie sleeves, feeling suddenly out of place among the polished marble and framed portraits of composers he couldn't name.

Then a voice carried across the empty hall.

"Mr. Blake."

Anton Weiss stood center stage, his posture as composed as ever, his tuxedo replaced by a dark turtleneck and quiet authority. His silver hair caught the overhead light, glinting like sheet music under a lamp.

"You came."

Aaron nodded awkwardly. "Yeah. I... figured I'd see what a rehearsal looks like."

Anton's expression didn't change, but a small smile touched his voice.

"Good. Curiosity is the beginning of understanding."

Aaron followed Anton down the aisle toward the stage. The orchestra was starting to assemble. The strings were tuning, a few brass players murmuring, a percussionist flexing their hands on a snare attempting to nimble up.

It sounded chaotic, but Anton didn't flinch. He stood still, baton at his side, eyes half-closed. He was simply *listening*.

To Aaron, it sounded like noise. To Anton, it was something else.

After a moment, Anton turned to him.

"Do you hear the shape of it?"

Aaron frowned. "Shape?"

Anton gestured toward the ensemble. "Every sound has structure. Even when they're not yet playing together, you can hear *intention*. The conductor's work begins before the music does."

He stepped onto the podium. Instantly, the room shifted. It

was like the gravity had realigned. The musicians straightened. The chatter quieted.

Anton raised his baton. Silence crystallized into attention.

Then. A gentle downbeat. And movement started.

The violins entered like breath. Cellos followed, rich and grounded. Brass entered last, soft but confident.

Aaron's eyes widened. What had been chaos seconds ago was now... coherence. Complete order. And utterly beautiful.

It wasn't just notes. It was coordination. Communication.

Anton guided with minimal gestures. A simple glance, a lift, a flick of his wrist. Yet with every gesture, the players responded as if they shared the same mind.

After a few minutes, he lowered his baton. The sound tapered off into stillness.

He turned toward Aaron.

"What did you see?"

Aaron hesitated. "You weren't telling them what to play."

Anton nodded. "Exactly. The score is already written. My job is to align the people who play it."

He stepped closer. "Tell me, Mr. Blake, when you design software, do you write every line yourself?"

Aaron shook his head. "No. I used to, but I just can't do that anymore. There are too many parts, too many moving pieces."

"And yet," Anton said, "you still believe your system should sound harmonious, yes?"

Aaron remembered the night before, and the aches and pains of the day. He smiled faintly. "That would be nice."

Anton leaned lightly on the conductor's stand. "Then you are not so different from me. The difference is only in the medium. You conduct systems of code; I conduct systems of sound."

He tapped the score lightly. "Both must live, breathe, and adapt. Both fail when one part ignores the rest."

The musicians resumed tuning. Aaron stood silently, absorbing it all. The hall felt alive. It was a network of moving parts, self-contained yet interconnected.

He thought of last night's pager call. The failing service, the ripple of impact across teams, the stress and agony. He saw it now, mirrored in the orchestra: one instrument slightly out of sync, throwing the whole composition off-balance.

Anton's voice cut through his thoughts.

"The architect," he said, "is the one who listens for imbalance before it becomes silence."

Aaron looked at him. "So, you're saying... architecture is about listening?"

Anton smiled. "Listening, awareness, alignment. The music is already in motion. You must decide whether to chase it. Or to guide it."

Aaron exhaled slowly. The fatigue he'd been carrying since 3 a.m. began to feel lighter. It wasn't gone, but it was... reframed.

He wasn't just tired. He was untuned.

Anton extended the baton toward him. "Come. Try it."

Aaron froze. "I, *what???*"

"Conduct them," Anton said simply. "They will follow if you listen first."

Aaron stared at the baton, hesitant. Then, slowly, he stepped onto the podium. The musicians looked up, curious. A few smiles appeared on their faces. He felt the weight of every eye on him.

He raised the baton.

For a heartbeat, the hall was silent.

And in that silence, Aaron realized something he hadn't understood until now:

> *Leadership doesn't begin when you move.*
> *It begins when you listen.*

♪ ♪ ♪

LESSON: THE ARCHITECT'S FIRST BATON

You'll want to control everything. *Don't.*

An architect doesn't control systems. They conduct them.

Architecture is the art of creating the conditions for coherence. A room where every service, every person, every decision can find its rhythm in the whole. You don't make that room by talking louder. You make it by listening first.

Listen to who's tuning. Listen to who's quiet. Listen to who's compensating for whom.

The conductor's most powerful tool is silence. So is yours.

When you stop trying to play every part, the people who actually play them start playing together.

That's what the baton is for.

Chapter 4

♪ *Systems as Symphonies* ♪

The next evening, Aaron arrived early.

The hall was the same. No audience. No applause. Just the low hum of the nearly empty hall.

Anton was already there, standing at the edge of the stage, studying the conductor's score under the glow of a single lamp.

He didn't look up.

"You came back."

Aaron nodded. "I'm not quite sure why."

Anton looked up at Aaron. "Curiosity, it's a good start.

"Sit."

Aaron dropped into the front row. His laptop bag slid down beside him like a loyal pet.

Anton turned a page on the stand. "Tell me, Mr. Blake. What did you *hear* last night?"

Aaron thought for a moment. "I heard..."

He thought some more.

"It was, like, everything depended on everything else. If one part drifted, the whole thing tilted."

Anton smiled. "Very good."

"Music and systems share a truth: both are fragile networks with complex interactions, pretending to be simple."He lifted the baton, tapping it lightly against the stand.

Music and systems share a truth: both are fragile networks with complex interactions, pretending to be simple.

Aaron tilted his head. "Are you saying complexity is normal?"

"I'm saying coherence is a miracle." Anton motioned toward the empty stage. "Imagine your orchestra as an application."

He gestured to invisible sections.

"The strings. Those are your core services. They provide the structure and flow of your application."

"The woodwinds. Those are your user interface, connecting to your audience."

"The brass. That's your infrastructure. They are loud and proud, yet utterly necessary. They give your application a solid foundation."

"The percussion. That's operations. They are always in the back, keeping time, keeping things moving forward. They are unnoticed until they stop."

Aaron smiled. "And the conductor?"

"The architect of course," Anton said. "The architect is responsible for harmony, not heroics."

> "The architect is responsible for harmony, not heroics."

He stepped off the podium and sat beside Aaron, lowering his voice.

"You write code, yes?"

Aaron nodded.

"You think in detail. In logic, syntax, precision. But an architect must think in motion. You must imagine how each part interacts *while* it plays."

Aaron frowned slightly. "That's hard. There's so much detail to keep in my head."

Anton's smile deepened. "Exactly. Which is why you stop keeping it in your head."

Pausing, he continued, "You must listen instead."

He tapped his temple. "A developer hears their own instrument." He then swept his hands broadly across the stage. "An architect hears the orchestra."

Aaron leaned forward. "So how do I start... listening?"

Anton folded his hands. "Ask the same questions I ask my musicians." He counted on his fingers:

1. "*What are you playing?*" They must understand their purpose.
2. "*Who are you playing with?*" Who are their dependencies? Who do they depend on, and who depends on them?
3. "*Can you hear each other?*" Are you communicating effectively with your dependencies?
4. "*Are you in tune?*" Each member must align with established standards and expectations.
5. "*Do you know when to stop?*" Do you know where your part fits into the whole? Do you understand restraint and constraints?

He looked at Aaron. "Ask those questions of every team and every system you touch."

Aaron chuckled softly. "That's... actually useful."

Anton nodded. "Architecture is useful, when it stops pretending to be mystical."

The musicians started filing in to begin their rehearsal. The cacophony of tuning and practicing instruments filled the room once more.

The rehearsal began.

Anton raised his baton, and the orchestra began again.

This time, however, the orchestra was practicing a more complex passage.

Anton whispered to Aaron, "Listen for imbalance."

Aaron closed his eyes. The violins were a bit sharp, the horns a fraction late, the flutes barely audible.

Anton leaned in. "Every imbalance tells a story. A system out of sync is never silent. Rather, it hums with tension. Your job is to hear that tension before it breaks."

Aaron opened his eyes. "And if it's already broken?"

Anton smiled faintly. "Then you fix it by *teaching them to listen to each other.* Not by yelling louder."

When the rehearsal ended, the musicians began packing up. Aaron remained seated, staring at the score.

Anton tapped the stand. "You look thoughtful."

"I just realized." Aaron said quietly. "At work, I'm always trying to play every instrument myself."

Anton turned to him. "Then stop."

Aaron looked up. *Was it really that simple?*

"The conductor doesn't play," Anton said. "He creates the conditions for others to play beautifully."

Aaron let out a slow breath. The idea felt both terrifying and liberating.

LESSON: THE ARCHITECT'S EAR

Developers hear features. Architects hear flow.

To think like an architect is to listen for *relationships*.

- Relationships between services.
- Relationships between people.
- Relationships between ideas.

You don't design perfection. You design balance.

When every part knows its purpose and timing, the system plays itself. That's harmony.

Harmony in music, harmony in software, harmony in life.

Part Two

Flow, Not Control

Chapter 5

♪ *The Dissonance* ♪

Monday morning.

Aaron stood by the whiteboard, marker in hand, surrounded by diagrams that only half-made sense. Boxes. Arrows. Lines connecting everything to everything else.

He'd come in early, eager. He was inspired by Anton's words, which still played in his head:

> *"You must imagine how each part interacts while it plays."*

Aaron had stayed up all night sketching a new architecture proposal that was cleaner, with fewer dependencies. It was *harmony through structure.*

Now he was ready to show it off to the rest of the team.

The team filtered in slowly, coffee cups in hand. Rachel joined last, sliding into a chair and raising an eyebrow.

"You've been busy," she said.

Aaron grinned. "I think I figured out a way to simplify the process. And maybe fix half our ongoing problems while we're at it."

"Ambitious," said Susan, the lead front-end developer. She stifled a yawn, not taking his comments seriously.

Aaron launched into his pitch. Diagrams. Flowcharts. He was full of energy and jazzed about what he was showing. He explained how their components could better communicate. He explained how latency could drop and how the new structure would make integration easier.

He explained how his idea was better than anything else, and how it solved *everything*!

Halfway through, he realized no one was really paying attention.

"So, wait" someone interrupted. "Are you saying we need to rewrite the *entire* backend queuing system?"

"Well, eventually, yes," Aaron said. "But if you think of it like an orchestra..."

An awkward silence.

Rachel bit her lip, holding back a giggle.

"An orchestra?" Priya said, skeptical. "Aaron, we're just trying to ship the release by Friday."

"I know, but if we coordinated the teams differently, we could..."

"Did management approve this?" someone asked.

Aaron hesitated. "Not yet. I wanted to show you all the idea first."

"And who's going to do the extra work?" another voice said. "We're already behind."

The room began to buzz. There was frustration and confusion. And inevitably, extreme resistance.

Aaron's heart beat faster...louder... He tried to pull the meeting back together. He raised his voice slightly. "Look, I'm not saying we rewrite everything overnight. Just...listen for a second. We're out of tune. Everyone's building great parts, but they don't fit together. They don't *resonate!*"

He looked around. Nope. Nothing but blank faces.

It was clear. The room didn't want a conductor. It simply wanted to get through the week.

♪ ♪ ♪

When the meeting ended, Rachel lingered.

"Well," she said gently, "that didn't exactly sing."

Aaron groaned, collapsing into his chair. "I sounded like a motivational poster."

"You sounded like someone trying too hard to fix everything all at once."

He rubbed his eyes. "I was just trying to help them see the big picture."

"They don't need to see the big picture. They need you to *hear* them first."

Aaron frowned. "I thought that's what I was doing."

Rachel smiled softly. "You were hearing *your* music, not theirs."

That night, Aaron sat alone at his desk long after everyone left.

His whiteboard symphony of boxes and arrows stared back at him. He saw it for what it *really* was, a silent mess.

He realized something Anton had said earlier:

> *"Every imbalance tells a story. Your job is to hear it before it breaks."*

He hadn't listened. Not really. He'd tried to *conduct noise,* not harmony.

♪ ♪ ♪

The next evening, Aaron returned to Benaroya Hall.

Anton was on stage again, mid-rehearsal. The orchestra sounded off. It was very slight, but Anton stopped mid-measure.

He didn't scold. He didn't raise his voice. He simply tapped his baton twice and said, "Let's find where we stopped listening."

Aaron felt that sentence like a punch.

When the musicians resumed, the difference was immediate. Subtle, but real. The music breathed again.

Anton caught Aaron's eye from across the hall.

"Rough day?" he asked later.

Aaron nodded. "I tried to apply what you said. It... didn't go well."

Anton smiled faintly. "Let me guess, you tried to conduct before you learned to listen."

Aaron sighed. "It's harder than it looks."

Anton's voice softened. "Leadership always is. A conductor without trust is just a man waving a stick."

Anton placed a hand on the music stand.

"Do you know the hardest part of leading an orchestra?"

Aaron shook his head.

"Convincing them it's *their* music, not yours."

He looked at Aaron steadily.

"When you return to your team, don't talk about *your* architecture. Ask about *their* challenges. Their tempo. Their needs. Then guide gently, in rhythm with them."

Aaron nodded slowly. "Guide, not dictate."

"Exactly. Teach them to listen to each other. Then, you will hear harmony."

LESSON: THE ARCHITECT'S HUMILITY

You cannot conduct what you do not understand.

You cannot lead what you do not listen to.

A great architect doesn't impose a vision. They reveal it, through the voices of the people who build it.

Systems, like orchestras, only follow leaders who *hear* before they speak.

And the music of leadership begins not with authority, but with awareness.

Chapter 6

♪ *The Bridge* ♪

The next morning, Aaron didn't rush to work.

He walked.

Seattle's morning was cool, dark, and wet. The city moved around him. Buses groaned, light rail bells rang, espresso machines hissed inside coffee shops on every corner.

He moved through the bustle, replaying Anton's words in his mind:

"Convincing them it's their music, not yours."

By the time he reached the office, he wasn't thinking about code anymore. He was thinking about connection.

Rachel was already ♪ there. Her headphones were on. She was sketching in her notebook.

Pixel, her cat, graced the cover of her laptop in sticker form, staring back at him disapprovingly.

Aaron dropped into the chair across from her.

She looked up. "Morning. You look... human again. That's progress."

He smiled faintly. "Barely. I stayed up thinking."

"Dangerous habit," she said. "Thinking."

He laughed quietly. "You were right yesterday. I was trying to conduct noise."

She set her pencil down. "That's not failure, Aaron. That's feedback."

For a moment, they sat in silence, only the type of silence that two good friends who've weathered the same storms could sit in.

Finally, Rachel said, "You know what your problem is?"

"I have several," Aaron said, thinking about all the truth in that statement.

"You think architecture is about control. It's not. It's about connection."

He frowned. "Connection."

She flipped her notebook around. Inside was a sketch. Not code, not design, but people. Teams, labeled like instruments: *Backend. Frontend. Product. Ops.* Arrows connected them, but not in straight lines, rather in arcs. Curved, flowing, musical.

"At work," she said, "you're trying to synchronize people by process. But people don't sync by process, they sync by purpose."

Aaron leaned forward. "So, you're saying architecture is emotional?"

She smiled. "Everything that matters **is** emotional."

He thought about Anton's orchestra. The way one raised bow could ripple through an entire section.

And Rachel's words clicked in.

"Anton listens for imbalance," Aaron said slowly. "You listen for resonance."

Rachel nodded. "Exactly. You can't make harmony without hearing how people *feel* inside the system you're building."

Aaron chuckled. "You sound like Anton now."

"Then he sounds smart," she said with a wink.

Rachel walked over to the whiteboard. She drew three overlapping circles labeled *Technology, Process,* and *People.*

She tapped the center. "That's where architecture lives. The intersection."

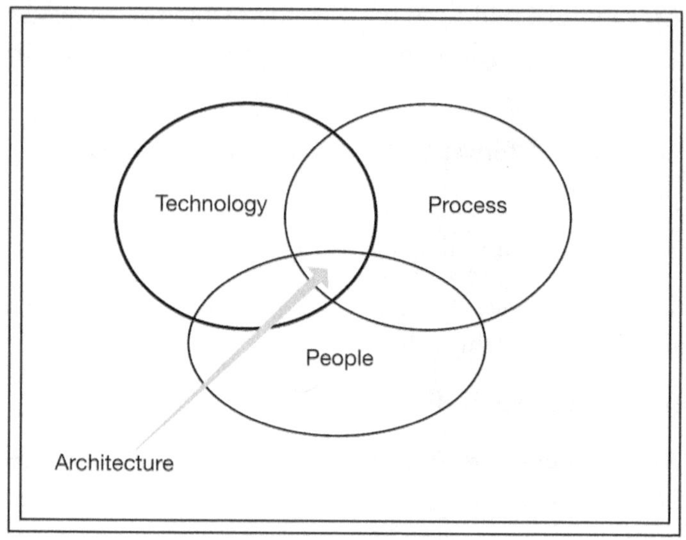

Aaron stared at it. "I've been ignoring one of those circles."

"Yeah," she said. "The human one."

He nodded slowly. "So how do I fix that?"

She smiled. "Start by asking what they need instead of telling them what they should do."

That night, Aaron returned to his apartment. The rain left reflections of streetlights rippling in the puddles.

He remembered something that Anton had said to him the day before.

"Every part must feel seen to play its best."

He wrote it down on a page in his notebook.

At the time Anton said it, Aaron didn't understand it.

But as Aaron stared at it, he started to get it.

He turned the page to a fresh page in his notebook. At the top, he wrote Anton's name, then next to it he wrote Rachel's. Below the names, he wrote simply:

"Architecture is empathy, at scale."

He didn't know it yet, but that one sentence would become the foundation of everything he built thereafter.

LESSON: THE ARCHITECT'S HEART

When a system fails, the code is rarely the first thing to look at.

Most failures in modern software aren't bugs. They're connections gone quiet. Between teams that stopped talking, between services whose owners no longer trust each other, between what an interface does and what the humans on either end actually need from it. The code is the symptom. The connection is the cause.

Architecture is empathy, at scale.

In practice that means listening for the human concern inside the technical objection. When a team pushes back on your design, the resistance is rarely about the design itself. It's about what the design will require them to carry, or change, or lose. When a developer says, "this feels wrong" and can't say why, sit with them until they can. The signal is almost always there before the symptom.

Stop telling people what to build. Start asking them what they need.

The diagram has three circles. The work is in the overlap.

Chapter 7

Interlude: Teacher not Dictator

~ Interlude ~

THE HERO TRAP

A common trap that someone new to the role of architect falls into is to assume that their job is to solve all the problems and tell everyone else what the solutions are.

Many outstanding developers operate in what can be called *"hero mode."* They become the person that everyone turns to when there's a problem to fix. If a project is falling behind, the hero developer is called in to bring it back on track. When the critical system goes down and the fix is non-obvious, the hero developer is called in to figure out what's wrong.

These hero developers are often the ones who are promoted into architectural leadership positions.

When entering a new role as software architect, it's natural to assume that the same skills that made you successful as a developer (and got you the promotion) are the same skills you should leverage in your new role. After all, isn't the architect the one ultimately responsible for making sure everything works in the system? If there is a problem in the system, it is the architect who is on the hook to explain what happened and solve the problem.

All of this tends to make the newly promoted architect assume the best way forward is to:

- Take all the data available to them
- Internalize it
- Solve the problem
- Broadcast the solution to everyone who needs to know

They get into a habit of simply "announcing" what the decisions are and what the architecture should look like, expecting everyone to move forward implementing the specified solution.

The software **architect** becomes more of a software **dictator**.

WHY DICTATING DOESN'T WORK

However, the best software architects know that this "hero" mindset won't take them very far. If a software architect simply goes around "dictating" answers to all the problems the team encounters, they will not be effective for long. Why? Well, there are several reasons:

Limited Perspective: If you always dictate the answer, all the answers will come from you. While you may know a lot, you don't know everything. Many great ideas will be lost because they didn't come from you.

Creating Bottlenecks: Others will start to assume you'll have all the answers and will come to you for all decisions. All decisions, including the ones they can clearly make on their own. You'll become a bottleneck, and you'll become overwhelmed simply by answering questions. The organization can't scale with bottlenecks such as this.

Preventing Knowledge Transfer: Being the central focus means that Knowledge will tend to stay localized with you. You will not be able to effectively communicate important knowledge across the organization. You become indispensable in a bad way. When you are not available, progress is hampered.

No Succession Planning: You will not be able to train the "next you." Who will take your place when you are ready to move on to a bigger and better role? If you make all the decisions, nobody else will be able to make those decisions if you were to move on.

THE TEACHING APPROACH

On the other hand, the role played by an outstanding architect could not be further from this dictator path. The best architects don't simply dictate the answer to the problem. Instead, they work *with* developers, helping them to understand the facts that lead to a solution, and helping the developers come to the right decisions on their own. They guide developers in making the right decisions. This results in decisions that are right for the application and the entire organization.

The best architects aren't dictators...they are teachers.

Educating developers rather than merely commanding them is the best way to encourage ownership and create a shared understanding of other teams' needs. The architect can't always be around. The more a team understands the needs and requirements of other groups, the better their decisions will be, and the better the application as a whole will perform.

The best architects know that they can't do everything by themselves. They need their team of developers to be motivated to work with them to solve problems. They need the expertise and experience of the entire team to find the best solutions. The best architects leverage the experience and skills of the entire team.

The architect trains, encourages, and funnels the energy of the development organization to improve the entire organization.

The best architects aren't *hero developers*. They are *catalysts* that build a cohesive team technically as well as architecturally. Architects, ultimately, make the entire organization better.

The best architects aren't *dictators*. They are teachers. They are mentors. They are catalysts that make the entire organization better.

Part Three

Mentoring and Coaching

Chapter 8

♪ *The Rehearsal Coach* ♪

The text arrived just after lunch.

Aaron stared at his phone. He'd been deep in a design review, half his attention on the whiteboard, the other half wondering if he'd ever stop second-guessing every architectural decision.

♪ ♪ ♪

The lobby smelled like fresh paint and ambition. Trophy cases lined the walls and championship banners hung from the rafters. Aaron felt distinctly out of place in his worn hoodie and jeans.

Anton appeared from a hallway, walking with his usual measured grace. "Ah, Mr. Blake. Right on time."

"Anton, what are we doing here?"

Anton's eyes held that familiar spark of mischief. "Learning."

They walked through corridors lined with photos of players mid-leap, mid-tackle, mid-triumph. Anton stopped at a glass door marked *COACHING STAFF*.

Inside, a man in his fifties sat reviewing game footage on multiple screens. He had the weathered look of someone who'd spent decades reading complex systems in real-time. Salt-and-pepper hair, sharp eyes, a coffee mug that read *TRUST THE PROCESS*.

He looked up when they entered. "Anton! Right on time." He stood, extending a hand. "You must be Aaron. I'm Marcus Chen. Offensive coordinator."

Aaron shook his hand, still confused. "Wow, it's a pleasure to meet you. I'm... not sure why I'm here."

Marcus laughed. "That's what I said when Anton called. But he's persuasive."

Anton settled into a chair. "Aaron is learning to think architecturally. I thought you might help him understand something I cannot."

Marcus raised an eyebrow. "What's that?"

"The difference between playing and coaching."

Understanding dawned on Marcus's face. He nodded slowly, then gestured for Aaron to sit. "Okay. Yeah, I can see it. Let me ask you something, Aaron. Do you know what my job is?"

Aaron glanced at the screens showing X's and O's in elaborate patterns. "You... design plays?"

"That's what people think." Marcus tapped one of the screens. "But designing plays is maybe twenty percent of what I do. The other eighty percent?" He leaned back. "I teach people how to see."

Aaron frowned. "See what?"

"The field. The game. Each other." Marcus pulled up footage, pausing on a single frame. "Look at this. Third down, seven yards to go. What do you see?"

Aaron studied the frozen moment. "Offensive line, quarterback, receivers..."

"That's what a fan sees," Marcus said. "A player sees their assignment. The quarterback sees the coverage. But you know what I see?"

He traced lines across the screen with his finger, connecting players, indicating spaces.

"I see time. I see decisions happening in sequence. I see who trusts who. I see where communication breaks down before it breaks down." He looked at Aaron. "I see the system."

Anton spoke quietly from his chair. "Go on."

Marcus stood, pacing slightly. "When I was playing, I was a quarterback. A pretty good one, actually. Full scholarship, couple of good years in college. And I thought I understood football."

He smiled, self-deprecating. "I understood *my* football. My reads, my progressions, my timing. But when I became a coach?" He shook his head. "I realized I'd been playing the game half-blind."

"What changed?" Aaron asked.

"I had to see through eleven sets of eyes instead of one." Marcus gestured to the field beyond the windows. "As a player, my job was execution. Read the defense, make the throw, move the chains. Simple. Hard, but simple."

He turned back to Aaron. "As a coach, my job is orchestration. I have to understand what the left tackle is seeing, what the receiver is thinking, whether the center and quarterback are in sync. I have to know if my running back is tired, if my tight end is frustrated, if my offensive line is starting to break down before they do."

Aaron felt something click. "You're designing for people, not plays."

"Exactly." Marcus sat on the edge of his desk. "A play is just a diagram. It's theory. But the moment it hits the field it becomes something else. It becomes improvisation within structure. It becomes eleven people interpreting the same idea in real-time while the other team tries to destroy it."

He pulled up another clip. "Watch this. Same play we just looked at. Fourth quarter, different game."

The play unfolded. The routes looked similar, but something was off. The timing was wrong. The quarterback held the ball too long. Pressure collapsed the pocket.

"What happened?" Marcus asked.

Aaron studied it. "The... rhythm was wrong?"

"Yes!" Marcus looked pleased. "The left guard missed his block by half a second. Just half a second. But that tiny delay cascaded. The running back had to adjust his route. The quarterback's timing got thrown. The receiver came open exactly when the quarterback was eating turf."

He paused the video. "As a player, I would've blamed the line. Or the back. Or myself. But as a coach, I see the whole system. And I see that the guard missed his block because we'd been pounding them with pass protection all game and he was exhausted. His technique was fine. His gas tank was empty."

Aaron leaned forward. "So what do you do?"

"I adjust. Maybe I call more running plays to give the line a breather. Maybe I substitute fresh legs. Maybe I change the protection scheme so he's not bearing the full load." Marcus smiled. "But here's the key: I don't do any of that unless I'm watching the whole field. Unless I'm seeing the system, not just the scoreboard."

Anton spoke again, his voice soft. "Tell him about trust."

Marcus nodded, his expression growing serious. "The hardest part of my job isn't designing plays. It's not studying film. It's not even managing egos, though that's tough enough."

He met Aaron's eyes. "The hardest part is letting go."

Aaron blinked. "Letting go?"

"Of control. Of perfection. Of the idea that I can execute the play for them." Marcus gestured to the field. "I can call the perfect play. I can prepare them perfectly. I can see everything developing exactly as it should. But when that ball is snapped, they're out there. Not me."

He walked to the window. "I had a receiver once. Talented kid. Fast, great hands. But he kept running the wrong routes. Not because he didn't know them, but because he was trying to fix what he thought were my mistakes in the play design."

"Was he right?" Aaron asked.

Marcus laughed. "Sometimes, yeah. He saw things I didn't. But the problem wasn't his insight, it was his timing. He'd improvise mid-play, and suddenly he'd be somewhere the quarterback didn't expect. Great idea, wrong execution."

"What did you do?"

"I taught him to trust the system first, then adjust. I told him, 'Run the play as called. If you see something, tell me after. We'll put it in the playbook. But you can't conduct the orchestra while you're playing the violin.'"

The phrase hung in the air. Anton smiled faintly.

"You can't conduct the orchestra while you're playing the violin.'"

Marcus turned back. "That's the thing about leadership, Aaron. You're trying to create something that's bigger than any individual can hold in their head. No single player can see the whole field. No single developer can understand every service. That's why you exist."

"To see it all," Aaron said slowly.

"To see it all," Marcus confirmed. "But more than that, to help them see each other. The best teams aren't the ones where the coach controls everything. They're the ones where the players trust the system enough to execute their part while trusting their teammates to execute theirs."

He pulled up one more clip. This time, the play unfolded beautifully. Quick snap, clean protection, precise routes, perfect throw, touchdown.

"Same play," Marcus said. "Different game. You know why it worked this time?"

Aaron watched it again. "Everyone did their job?"

"Close. Everyone *trusted* everyone else to do their job. Watch the left tackle. He doesn't hold his block too long. He knows the ball's coming out quick. Watch the receiver. He doesn't round off his route looking for the ball. He trusts the timing. Watch the quarterback. He throws before the receiver comes open because he trusts the receiver will be there."

Marcus paused. "That's architecture. That's coaching. That's conducting. Whatever you want to call it. You're not building a machine where every gear turns exactly as programmed. You're building a system of people who trust each other enough to be brilliant together."

Aaron sat back, absorbing it. "So how do you build that trust?"

"You start by showing them you see them," Marcus said. "Not as functions in your playbook, but as people with strengths, weaknesses, fears, ambitions. You learn who needs encouragement and who needs honesty. Who thrives under pressure and who needs preparation. Who's playing hurt and trying to hide it."

He gestured at the screens. "I can draw up the most brilliant play in the world. But if I don't know my people, it's just lines on paper. The play doesn't work because it's clever. It works because it fits the players I have, in the moment I have them."

Anton finally stood. "Aaron, do you understand what Marcus is saying?"

Aaron nodded slowly. "Architecture isn't about designing the perfect system. It's about designing the system that works for the people who have to build and maintain it."

"And?" Anton prompted.

"And... I can't do that unless I understand them. Not just their skills, but who they are."

Marcus smiled. "Now you're getting it. You know what the best coaches have in common? They were all players once. They remember what it feels like to be on the field, exhausted, confused, with everything moving too fast. They remember needing someone who could see the whole picture when they could only see their assignment."

He moved toward the door. "Come on. Practice is starting. Let me show you something."

They walked out to the edge of the practice field. Players were stretching, jogging, going through warm-up drills. Marcus stood with his arms crossed, not yelling, not directing, just watching.

"See him?" Marcus pointed to a linebacker. "He's favoring his left leg. Probably tweaked it yesterday. He won't say anything because he doesn't want to lose his starting spot. I'll pull him aside later, make sure he's okay, maybe adjust our defensive scheme to take some load off him."

He pointed to a receiver. "That guy's having relationship trouble. I can tell by how he's running routes. His head's not in it. I'll check in with him after practice."

Aaron watched the players move through their drills. Dozens of people, each with their own concerns, their own pressures, their own fears and dreams. And Marcus saw them all.

"You can't coach people you don't know," Marcus said quietly. "And you can't know them if you don't look. Really look. Not at their stats or their performance metrics. At *them*."

A whistle blew. The team gathered. Marcus jogged over, and Aaron watched him move through the group. A word here, a pat on the shoulder there, a joke that made someone laugh, a serious conversation with another.

Anton stood beside Aaron. "See the difference?"

"Between playing and coaching?"

"Between controlling and conducting."

Aaron watched Marcus call a play, watched the team execute it, watched him stop them, make an adjustment, try again. It looked like chaos but felt like purpose.

"He's not trying to win practice," Aaron said.

"No," Anton agreed. "He's trying to teach them how to win the game. And he can only do that by understanding what they need to succeed."

They stood in silence for a while, watching the practice unfold.

Finally, Aaron said, "I've been thinking about architecture wrong."

Anton glanced at him. "How so?"

"I've been thinking of it as design. As plans and patterns and principles. But it's not really about that, is it?"

"Tell me what it's about."

Aaron watched Marcus crouch down next to a rookie who'd run the wrong route, watched him draw something in the dirt, watched the player's face light up with understanding.

"It's about people," Aaron said. "The architecture is just the language we use to help them work together. But if I don't understand them, if I don't see what they need, what they're struggling with, what they're capable of..." He trailed off.

"Then you're just drawing diagrams," Anton finished.

Aaron nodded. "Just waving the baton."

They both smiled.

♪ ♪ ♪

Later, as they walked back to the parking lot, Aaron's mind churned with thoughts.

"Anton, can I ask you something?"

"Of course."

"Why Marcus? Why a football coach?"

Anton smiled. "Because orchestras can feel abstract to you. Beautiful, but distant. But you understand sports. You watch football. You see the strategy, the execution, the pressure."

He paused at his car. "And because Marcus understands something crucial that many architects miss."

"What's that?"

"That your team isn't your instrument. They're your orchestra. And the best you can do is create the conditions for them to play brilliantly together. You cannot play for them. You cannot score the touchdown for them. You can only see what they cannot, show them how their individual excellence contributes to collective success, and trust them to execute."

Aaron unlocked his car, then hesitated. "What if they don't execute? What if they fail?"

"Then you learn," Anton said simply. "You adjust. You try again. Just like Marcus does. Just like every conductor does when the orchestra misses a cue." He opened his door. "The question is not whether they will fail. They will. Everyone does. The question is whether you will see the failure as *their* failure, or as information about how to better design the system."

Aaron sat in his car for a long time after Anton drove away.

He thought about his team. About the last time he'd really looked at them, not at their code or their velocity or their ticket counts, but at *them*. Who was struggling? Who needed encouragement? Who had potential they weren't using because they didn't believe they could?

He pulled out his phone and started making notes:

Talk to Sarah about her concerns with the API design. She's been quiet in meetings.

Check in with Dave. He's been taking on too much. Probably burning out.

Ask the team what they need from me. Not what I think they need. What they actually need.

His phone buzzed. A text from Rachel:

RACHEL:

How was the mystery meeting?

He started the engine, but before pulling out, he looked back at the training facility. Through the fence, he could see players still running drills, Marcus still watching, still adjusting, still teaching.

Architecture wasn't about control.

It was about creating the conditions for success.

It was about seeing the whole system.

It was about trusting your team enough to let them play.

And it was about understanding that you couldn't succeed without them.

♪ ♪ ♪

LESSON: THE ARCHITECT AS COACH

The developer plays one position. The architect coaches the entire team.

Your job is not to be the best player. Your job is to help everyone else become better players.

You cannot execute the code for them. You cannot make every decision. You cannot be in every meeting or understand every detail. But you can see patterns they cannot see.

You can identify problems before they cascade. You can create structures that help them succeed.

Architecture is not about knowing everything. It's about seeing everyone.

The best systems are not built by the smartest architect. They're built by teams who trust each other enough to be brilliant together.

And that trust begins with a leader who understands that their success depends entirely on the success of the people they serve.

You are not the player trying to win the game alone.

You are the coach creating the conditions for the whole team to win together.

Chapter 9

Interlude: Training and Mentoring

One of the hardest tasks for anyone is to train themselves out of a job. The natural insecurities about job security make this challenge even more difficult. Yet, as a software architect, training and growing the technical skills of your team is one of your major responsibilities. As the architect for a major application, you're responsible for the growth and training of the engineers working on that application whether you directly train them or not.

Upleveling the skills of your team to meet the needs for building and maintaining your application is a constant, ongoing process. You'll inevitably become a mentor for less experienced engineers and help guide their career growth paths. Even if you aren't directly involved in day-to-day training and mentoring, you'll be directing and determining the overall skillsets needed for the entire team, working on plans to ensure everyone has the necessary training and skills, and identifying where skill gaps exist to help create plans to fill those gaps.

THE ARCHITECT AS TEAM DEVELOPER

With team growth and training, you become a natural extension of the management team. The responsibility for the technical maturity of the organization rests in your hands.

You assess what the team can do, identify what they'll need, work with management on a plan to close the gap.

When the gap can't be closed, you adjust the architecture instead. This responsibility comes as a natural outcome of selecting the technologies and systems you'll utilize in your architecture design. If you're designing a system requiring a highly interactive front end, you need sufficiently trained front-end engineers capable of building that system. If your group doesn't have the right skill sets, you need to ensure the team acquires those skills. If not, then you need to rethink your architecture requirements.

Thinking Toward the Future

Besides considering the skills your application team needs today you must figure out and understand what skills they'll need in the future as your application grows and expands. You need to get ahead of the team's training to fill those future skill gaps. The specific skills will change with the era. The question doesn't.

Working as an Extension of Management

Your close relationship with both the development team and the management team puts you in a unique position. When management makes decisions that impact the development team, you're responsible for being an advocate of those decisions to the rest of the development organization. It doesn't matter whether or not you personally agree with them.

Whether or not it's a formal responsibility, you're a de facto mentor for all the engineers in your charge. You're a natural technical coach for those engineers. You must not only ensure the right decisions are made to improve the application, but you must also communicate those decisions to the team, explain your reasoning to those asking, and use every interaction as a tool to teach and grow the technical understanding, and ultimately the shared vision, for the team as a whole.

YOUR LEGACY: GROWING FUTURE ARCHITECTS

Perhaps the most important aspect of your training and mentoring role is growing engineers into becoming future architects. As your applications and organization grow and expand, this becomes just as important to your company as the systems you're building today.

A great architect is always trying to work themselves out of a job by growing their team to make decisions for themselves. This might seem counterintuitive, but it's the mark of true leadership. When you successfully train your team, you don't diminish your value, you multiply it. You create a culture of architectural thinking throughout your organization, and you develop the next generation of leaders who will take your systems and your company even further than you could alone.

Chapter 10

♪ *The Counterpoint* ♪

The coffee shop at the corner of First and Pine had become something between a meeting room and a confessional for Aaron and Rachel. Same booth, every time. The one by the window, where the steam from the espresso machine fogged the glass and the rain made the streetlights bloom into watercolor.

Aaron got there first. He ordered her usual chamomile and his green tea with ginger. Set them down on the table and waited.

When Rachel walked in, he could tell something was off before she even sat down.

She didn't lead with a joke. She didn't tease him about his hoodie or his hair or the way he was hunched over his phone. She just slid into the booth, wrapped both hands around her mug, and exhaled.

"Long one?" Aaron asked.

"Long week."

He waited. With Rachel, that usually worked.

After a minute she said, "I have a pitch tomorrow. A big one."

"How big?"

"The whole engineering org. I'm trying to land a redesign of the customer onboarding flow, and the entire backend team thinks it's..."

She made air quotes with her fingers.

"...lipstick."

Aaron winced. He knew that word. He'd used it himself, once, about a designer's mockup, before he understood what mockups actually represented.

"What do they want it to be?" he asked.

"I don't know. They want it to be code, I guess. They want it to ship. They don't want to talk about *why* we're shipping it."

"And you do."

"I have to. If I don't make the case, the whole redesign gets cut and we ship the thing we already know is broken. Again."

She set the mug down. He noticed her hand was shaking, just slightly. Rachel didn't get nervous. Rachel was the steady one. The one who walked into rooms full of opinions and walked out with the room.

"Hey," he said, gently. "What's actually going on?"

She didn't look up. "I've done this pitch three times. To three different audiences. Every time I do it, I lose them halfway through. I keep getting more emphatic, and the more emphatic I get the more they tune out, and by the end I'm basically yelling at a slide deck."

He almost laughed. Not because it was funny. But because he'd lived this. Recently. Painfully.

"I know exactly what you're describing," he said.

"Yeah?"

"It's the Monday morning whiteboard meeting. Remember I tried to redo our entire backend queuing system as a single elegant proposal and I lost the room before I got to slide three."

She smiled, remembering the meeting.

"I sat at my desk that night and stared at the whiteboard for two hours and felt like an idiot."

Rachel finally smiled. A small one, but a real one. "And then?"

"And then someone told me I was hearing my own music, not theirs."

She looked at him. He held her eyes.

"Oh," she said quietly. "That's... yeah. Yeah."

He waited. She picked up her mug again and turned it in her hands.

"Tell me about engineering," he said. "Not what you want them to hear. Tell me what they're actually saying."

She paused and organized her thoughts. "They're saying that they have three quarters of tech debt to address. They're saying that they can't take on a redesign right now, that the backend team is already two engineers short and the new hire ramps up next month. They're saying that every time design comes to them with a 'small' redesign it ends up being a six-month project that touches forty services. They're saying they are tired."

"OK," Aaron said. "What are *you* saying?"

"That the current onboarding is killing us. We have data that shows it. Drop-off, complaints, churn."

"Right, so you have facts. They have fatigue. Those two things don't argue with each other. They just talk past each other."

Rachel set down her mug. "Keep going."

"Anton told me once that the conductor's job is not to convince the orchestra to play his music. It's to find the music that's already in the room and bring it forward."

He paused. He hadn't realized he'd been carrying that line around like a coin in his pocket until he heard himself say it.

"You don't have a pitch problem," he said. "You have a *who's-already-on-your-side* problem."

"What does that mean?"

"It means there are engineers in that room who agree with you. Maybe not on the redesign, but on the *problem*. They're tired because they're maintaining a system they hate. The onboarding flow is part of why they're tired. If you walk in tomorrow and pitch the redesign, you're asking them to take on more work. If you walk in tomorrow and pitch the *problem*, you're handing them a way out of the work they already hate."

Rachel stared at him.

"Don't pitch the redesign," he said. "Pitch the pain. Then ask them what *they'd* do about it."

She didn't say anything for a long moment.

Then she said, "Aaron Blake. When did you become the smart one in this conversation?"

"I'm not. I'm the one who failed the same pitch three weeks ago. I just had a pretty good teacher."

"Anton."

"And you."

She blinked.

"You're the one who told me to stop trying to conduct noise," he said. "You drew the three circles. You said architecture lives in the intersection of technology, process, and people. I didn't make that up. I just borrowed it."

"You're giving me my own advice back."

"I'm trying to. With interest."

Rachel laughed, finally. A real one. The kind that loosened

something in her shoulders that had clearly been wound for days.

"Pixel's gonna be mad that I'm not home," she said.

"Pixel's a cat. Pixel is *always* mad you exist."

"Fair."

She pulled her notebook out of her bag, the same one with the sticker on the cover, and flipped to a blank page. Started writing.

He didn't read over her shoulder. He just sipped his tea and watched the rain bloom on the window.

After a few minutes she looked up. "Hey."

"Yeah?"

"Thanks for letting me be the one who needed help, for once."

He shrugged. "It was overdue."

She started to argue, but then didn't.

Outside, the rain lifted just enough that the streetlight stopped blooming and became a streetlight again. Aaron pulled out his phone, checked the time.

"You're going to land it tomorrow," he said.

"I might."

"You will."

"How do you know?"

"Because you're not going to walk in there trying to play

their instruments for them. You're going to walk in and listen. And then you're going to lift the baton."

She smiled. "Now you're just showing off."

"A little."

They sat there. They didn't say much else. The shop was quiet enough that Aaron could hear the espresso machine click off, then on again, then off, like a metronome that had given up keeping time and was just keeping company.

Outside, Seattle did its Seattle thing.

Inside, a designer wrote her pitch.

And the architect, for the first time, watched someone he cared about work something out without trying to work it out for her.

LESSON: THE COUNTERPOINT

The mentor and the mentored are not fixed roles.

A great architect doesn't just *receive* lessons. They reflect them back. They take what they were given, and they hand it forward. They hand it to colleagues, to teammates, to the people in their lives who are stuck in the same room they were stuck in last week.

This is how knowledge actually moves. Not through documents. Not through handbooks. Through a conversation in a coffee shop, where someone says, "I know exactly what you're describing," and means it.

You cannot become a conductor alone. You become one by

trading the baton, when the moment calls for it, with the people who taught you how to hold it.

74

Part Four

The Big Picture

Chapter 11

♪ *The Crescendo* ♪

The problem began with a message at 10:47 a.m.

A single red banner across the company's product status dashboard:

SERVICE UNAVAILABLE

At first, Aaron thought it was a false alarm. Then Slack lit up. The ops channel buzzed. The product channel. The management channel. He was getting direct messages from managers left and right, including managers he barely knew. They were trying to page everyone they could think of.

The database was failing, again. Replication lag, cascading retries, requests stacking up, waiting and unfulfilled.

Half the system was down. The other half was in the process of failing.

And nobody knew what to do. But they all knew that Aaron needed to fix it fast.

Aaron's pulse quickened. The familiar instinct kicked in. He opened the laptop to dig into the problem, find the failure, and fix it. After all, only he knew how it all worked. He needed to fix it quickly...yet again.

Yet again...sigh.

But this time, he stopped. He heard Anton's voice in his head:

> *"You cannot conduct what you do not understand.*
> *You cannot lead what you do not listen to."*

He took a deep breath. He stepped back from his keyboard. Instead, he moved his cursor over to the Ops channel and typed:

"Let's gather. Five minutes. War room."

♪ ♪ ♪

The conference room filled quickly. Engineers, managers, designers, support. Everyone was talking all at once.

Aaron stood by the whiteboard, marker in hand, feeling the noise surge like the untuned orchestra.

Rachel slipped in quietly, a tea in her hand. She gave him a nod. He took it as his cue...his conductor's cue.

He tapped the board once. "Let's find where we stopped listening."

The room went silent, quizzical looks abound.

"Okay," he said, steady now. "Ops, what do we know?"

"Replication lag. Reads are fine, writes are backing up."

"Frontend?"

"Users are stuck in infinite spinners. We're getting error floods!"

"Product?"

"Customer support is melting down. They want an ETA."

Aaron nodded. "Okay. Everyone, listen carefully. We're not fixing the code right now. We're fixing *the flow*."

He drew a quick sketch on the whiteboard: boxes for services, arrows for connections. The diagram looked eerily like Anton's score pages.

"Ops, throttle writes for now. Let's keep the system breathing as much as we can.

"Frontend, show an error state. Make it clear and calm, not panic. We need to show that we know what we are doing.

"Product, talk to customer support and tell them we're on it, no promises yet.

"Everyone else, stay synced here. No silos."

Someone started to object, "But we can't..."

Aaron raised a hand gently. "We'll get there. Let's align first."

Minutes passed. Then an hour.

The chaos began to thin. The tone in the room shifted. It was less noise, more rhythm. People started updating each other unprompted, cross-checking changes before deploying.

Aaron wasn't fixing the problem himself. Everyone was working together to solve the problem.

At one point, a junior developer caught a cascading rollback before it hit production. Aaron smiled.

"Nice catch," he said. "That's harmony."

Two hours later, the dashboard flickered from red to green.

Applause rippled through the room. Tired, relieved laughter following close behind.

Aaron leaned back in his chair, exhaling for what felt like the first time all day. He returned to his desk.

Rachel followed him to his desk, set her empty teacup down. "You didn't touch the keyboard once."

He smiled. "First time."

She grinned. "Anton would be proud."

He looked at her. "You think so?"

Rachel nodded. "You didn't just fix a system. You conducted one. You taught them all to work together and trust each other."

♪ ♪ ♪

After Rachel went back to her desk, Aaron sat with his laptop closed for a long moment. He realized he hadn't talked to Marcus since the practice field. He pulled out his phone.

Marcus picked up on the second ring. "Aaron."

"Coach."

"You sound tired."

"I'm not. That's the weird part."

There was a small pause on the other end, then a quiet laugh. "Tell me what happened."

Aaron told him. Not the technical version, after all, Marcus didn't care about replication lag. Aaron told him the people version. Who he'd called into the room. Who he'd kept out. The moment he'd watched his hand move toward the keyboard and stopped it. The junior developer who'd caught the rollback. The dashboard going green.

When he was done, the line was quiet for a beat.

"You let them play," Marcus said.

"I let them play."

"Then you did your job."

Aaron stood and walked to the window. Outside, the rain had started up again, soft and patient.

"Anton called me yesterday," Marcus said.

Aaron blinked. "He did?"

"Said you'd had a long week, and that something was probably coming. Wouldn't tell me what. Just said to keep my phone on."

Aaron almost laughed. "He's annoying like that."

"He is. He's also right a lot." A pause. "Are you on your way to see him?"

"How'd you know?"

"Because that's what you do after you win one. You go find your conductor." A car door closed somewhere on Marcus's end. "When you see him, tell him the rookie is ready."

Aaron felt something catch in his chest.

"Thanks, Coach."

"Don't thank me yet. You're just getting started."

The line went dead. Aaron looked at the phone for a long moment, then slid it into his pocket. He looked at his watch and reached for his coat. It was time to head down to see Anton.

♪ ♪ ♪

Aaron walked down to Benaroya Hall. The rehearsal had ended, the lights dimmed, the stage empty.

Anton sat alone in the front row, coat folded beside him, staring at the silent instruments.

Aaron approached quietly.

"It's funny," he said. "When you're in the middle of it, everything feels like noise. But if you stop trying to fix it, and just... listen. Then it starts to make sense."

Anton turned, smiling softly. "And what did you hear?"

Aaron thought for a moment. "People. Working in time with each other."

Anton nodded. "Then you are no longer a player. You are a conductor."

Anton stood up, quietly, and started walking away.

After a few steps, he stopped. "You learned something today." He was still facing away, the way he was walking.

Aaron looked at him. "What's that?"

"That leadership," Anton said, "is not performance. It's presence."

Anton continued walking away.

When Aaron left the hall that night, the rain had returned. This time it felt more cleansing and less cold.

He didn't feel tired anymore. His head was clear.

He looked at the city lights reflected in the puddles and thought of his team. He thought about the rhythm they'd found together, the system breathing again.

It wasn't perfect. But it was alive.

And for the first time, he understood what Anton had meant when he said:

> *"The conductor doesn't make the music. He creates the space where music can happen."*

LESSON: THE ARCHITECT'S BATON

The architect's power is not in control. The architect's power is in creating clarity.

When systems fail, people look for heroes. But what they really need is harmony.

An architect doesn't fix every note. They restore the rhythm that lets others play again.

Leadership is less about knowing all the answers and more about keeping the tempo when everyone else loses the beat.

Chapter 12

Interlude: The Architect's Vision (Big Picture vs Little Picture)

One of the most fundamental challenges facing a new architect is recognizing that the scope of their responsibility has fundamentally changed. You no longer have the freedom to focus on a single aspect of an application. An essential skill for a developer, focus often becomes inappropriate, and frankly impossible to achieve, as an architect.

This shift from little picture to big picture thinking defines the architectural role more than any other single characteristic. Understanding this shift, embracing it, and learning to operate effectively at this different level of abstraction is critical to your success as an architect.

THE ORCHESTRA METAPHOR REVISITED

Consider again the orchestra. When you're playing an instrument, such as the violin, you must understand deeply how to play that instrument. You must understand the music you're expected to play, and you must interpret the conductor's instructions to know when to play the different parts of the composition before you.

As the conductor, you understand what it takes to play the violin, along with all the other instruments in the orchestra. You may have even played the violin yourself, or perhaps other instruments. But you don't need to know in great detail the specifics involved in playing the violin's part.

Instead, you need to know how the violin's part fits into the whole. You need to lead everyone in the orchestra, giving them the instructions they all need to play together, synchronized, creating beautiful music.

The conductor is the architect. The individual instrument players are the developers.

Developers must understand one component, or at most a few components, to a deep level of understanding. As an architect, you must keep many distinct components and concepts in your mind simultaneously, maintaining a working knowledge of how they all function together. You won't have the level of detail knowledge that the developer does, but you'll have breadth of knowledge. Your focus becomes the big picture of the overall application, not just a single component or module.

DEEP VERSUS BROAD: A DIFFERENT KIND OF KNOWLEDGE

This represents a fundamental trade-off between depth and breadth:

The developer's knowledge is deep. They dive into the implementation details of their component. They understand every function, every edge case, every optimization opportunity within their domain. They know the intimate details of how their code works and why specific decisions were made.

The architect's knowledge is broad. They maintain surface-level expertise across many areas. They understand what each component does, how it fits into the system, and how it interacts with other components. But they don't necessarily know the implementation details of any single component.

The developer has narrow exposure to various concepts. They focus intensely on the specific service, module, or component that is their specific area of responsibility.

The architect has wide exposure to various concepts. They must understand development, operations, product requirements, business obligations, system scaling, and system health. Everything.

This difference in knowledge style isn't a weakness, it's a necessity. For the architect to be successful, they need shallow knowledge and wide exposure. The architect must depend on the deep knowledge and expertise of the software developers responsible for each component. You can't know everything about everything. Trying to maintain that depth across all components would be impossible and would pull you away from your actual responsibilities.

THE NATURE OF ARCHITECTURAL DECISIONS

This difference in knowledge style leads to a difference in how decisions get made.

Developers make many small decisions rapidly. Each day, a developer might make dozens or even hundreds of small technical choices. Which function should I call at this point in the code? How do I structure this data? What variable name should I use? These decisions happen quickly because the scope is limited and the context is well understood.

Architects make fewer but larger decisions more slowly. Architectural decisions have broader impact and require more consideration. These decisions happen at a slower cadence because they need input from multiple stakeholders, consideration of multiple perspectives, and careful evaluation of long-term consequences.

The software developer can be quick and decisive because they're operating with complete information within a narrow domain. The software architect must be slower and more deliberate because they're operating with incomplete information across a broad domain.

UNDERSTANDING CROSS-COMPONENT IMPACT

As an architect, when one development team determines they want to make a change to a component they own, it becomes your responsibility to understand the impact of that change beyond the scope of that single component.

You need to understand enough about all components of the system to determine if a desired change will require changes to other parts of the system. Then you must ensure the teams that own those other components understand the needed changes, have the time to implement them, and have the necessary skills and resources to do the work successfully.

THE INTERCONNECTION OF COMPONENTS

As you move from developer to architect, your scope of responsibility expands from a single component to the interconnection of a large number of components.

This interconnection is where the real complexity lives in modern applications. Individual components might be relatively simple, especially in a service and microservice-based architecture. But the interactions between those components become increasingly complex as the number of components grows.

Consider a system with ten microservices. There are potentially forty-five unique interactions between those services (each service might interact with any other service). Add just five more services to reach fifteen total, and you now have one hundred and five potential interactions. The complexity grows with the number of components.

This interconnection complexity typically isn't owned or understood by individual service teams. Individual teams' focus is on the services they're responsible for. The overall interaction complexity (and hence the application complexity as a whole) shows up in the relationships between teams, not within teams.

Who owns this interaction complexity? Usually, the software architects. It's typically your responsibility as an architect to understand and manage the complex interactions between services and systems.

A DIFFERENT LEVEL OF ABSTRACTION

The word "focus" takes on a whole new meaning as an architect. You're no longer focusing on the in-depth technical aspects of a single module. Instead, you focus on the wide-ranging interaction between multiple disparate systems.

It is still a type of focus, but it's a broader coverage area that you are responsible for, operating at a higher level of understanding. You're working at a different level of abstraction, thinking about problems in fundamentally different ways than you did as a developer.

This shift in abstraction level means:

You see patterns rather than details. Where a developer sees specific implementations, you see architectural patterns and design approaches. Where they see individual functions, you see component responsibilities and boundaries.

You think in terms of capabilities rather than implementations. You care less about how something is implemented and more about what capabilities it provides and how those capabilities fit into the larger system.

You evaluate trade-offs at the system level. Where a developer optimizes for their component, you optimize for the system as a whole. Sometimes this means accepting suboptimal decisions in individual components to achieve better system-wide outcomes.

You operate in longer time horizons. Developers often think in sprints and releases. Architects think in quarters and years, considering how today's decisions will impact the system's evolution over time.

THE CHALLENGE OF CONTEXT SWITCHING

Operating at this level of abstraction requires you to work in what might feel like an unfocused environment with constant interruptions and context changes.

As a developer, you could block out several hours to dive deep into a problem. You'd minimize distractions, close Slack, put on headphones, and achieve flow state where you're completely immersed in the code.

As an architect, you might start your morning discussing database scaling strategies, move to a meeting about API design standards, review a proposal for a new service, help a developer understand cross-service error handling, meet with product management about upcoming features, and then discuss operational concerns with the infrastructure team. Each of these requires different context, different knowledge, and different stakeholders.

This constant context switching can feel exhausting and unproductive, especially if you're used to the deep-focus work of software development. Nevertheless, it's a feature of the role of software architect. Your value comes from your ability to connect these disparate concerns, to understand how the database scaling conversation relates to the API design standards, and how both affect the new service proposal.

Learning to operate effectively with these constant context switches is one of the most important skills you'll develop as an architect. You can't eliminate the switching as it's inherent to the role. But you can become more efficient at it, maintaining enough context about each area to engage meaningfully without needing to load the complete deep context each time.

THE SHIFT IN MINDSET

Moving from developer to architect requires a fundamental mindset shift. You're no longer responsible for just writing a section of code. You're responsible for understanding and driving the technical aspects of the entire application.

You become an extension of the management team. You're the technical leader, the technical conductor, of the entire application organization. The entire application *orchestra*.

This shift can be disorienting. As a developer, you had clear boundaries around your responsibilities. You knew exactly what you were accountable for. As an architect, those boundaries become much fuzzier. Your responsibility touches everything, yet you don't directly control most of it.

Management and other developers will look to you for external knowledge and systemic understanding. They expect you to see things they can't see from their individual positions within the system. They expect you to connect dots that seem unrelated to them but that you understand are deeply interconnected.

WORKING IN THE BIG PICTURE

Operating effectively in the big picture requires specific practices:

Deliberately maintain broad context. Stay connected to what's happening across the organization. Attend standups for different teams. Review designs even for components you're not directly responsible for. Read postmortems from incidents in other areas. This broad awareness lets you spot connections and potential issues that others miss.

Build mental models of the system. You can't hold all the details in your head, but you can maintain working models of how things fit together. These models don't need to be perfectly accurate. Rather they need to be useful for reasoning about changes and understanding impacts.

Cultivate relationships across boundaries. Your effectiveness depends on your ability to work with people across the organization. Build relationships with developers, operations engineers, product managers, and business leaders. These relationships become the channels through which you gather information and influence decisions.

Develop pattern recognition. As you see more systems and more decisions, you'll start recognizing patterns. Some patterns will be successful and should be encouraged. Others are not and should be avoided. Recognizing the difference becomes one of your most valuable capabilities.

Know when to dive deep and when to stay high-level. You can't and shouldn't try to understand everything deeply. But you need to recognize the critical decisions that require deeper investigation versus the ones where high-level understanding suffices.

THE BALANCE

The big picture versus little picture distinction isn't absolute. Good architects don't completely abandon detail work. Instead, they're selective about when and where they engage with details.

Sometimes you need to dive into code to understand a performance problem. Sometimes you need to review detailed implementation plans to spot subtle issues. Sometimes you need to prototype solutions to validate architectural approaches.

The difference is that as an architect, these deep dives are exceptions rather than the rule. They're purposeful excursions to gather specific information or solve particular problems, not your primary mode of operation.

Your default mode *is* the big picture. The little picture work serves your big picture responsibilities rather than being the end goal itself.

EMBRACING THE SHIFT

The transition from little picture to big picture thinking is challenging. It requires you to let go of the satisfaction that comes from solving detailed technical problems and embrace the different satisfaction that comes from enabling others to solve those problems while ensuring the overall system remains coherent.

It requires you to accept that you won't be the expert in everything anymore. Your expertise shifts from knowing how to implement specific solutions to knowing how to ensure the right solutions get implemented across the entire system.

It requires you to become comfortable with ambiguity and incomplete information. You'll make important decisions without having all the data you'd like. You'll guide teams through complex problems where there's no clearly right answer.

But this shift also unlocks new capabilities. You can influence outcomes at a scale that's impossible as an individual contributor. You can shape how entire organizations build software. You can create systems that last for years and serve millions of users.

The big picture is where architects live.

Chapter 13

Interlude: Reviewing Ideas, Managing Churn

Architecture is not a static blueprint created once and followed forever. Modern applications exist in a state of constant evolution. Customer expectations shift. Business requirements change. New technologies emerge. The architecture that perfectly served your needs six months ago may already be outdated.

As an architect, managing this constant churn becomes one of your core responsibilities. You're not just designing systems. You're continuously evaluating, refining, and evolving those designs in response to feedback from all directions.

ARCHITECTURE IS FLUID, NOT FIXED

Architecting a modern application is not simply drawing up some diagrams and watching developers build what those pictures describe. The collaboration between you and your stakeholders (developers, product managers, operations engineers, upper management, and customers) never ends. This ongoing dialogue drives architectural decisions throughout the application's entire lifecycle.

The application architecture, like the code that supports it, is fluid and evolving. Modern architecture cannot be stagnant. It must constantly adapt to meet the needs of the business, the customers, and the teams building and operating the product.

Building a successful modern application architecture means constantly and incrementally improving it based on feedback from various stakeholders. This requires an architecture development process that embraces change rather than resisting it.

THE AGILE ARCHITECTURE CYCLE

The same agile principles that guide modern software development apply equally to architecture. You continuously loop through four key activities:

Gather Feedback and Evaluate. You must be constantly listening. Feedback comes from developers struggling with implementation challenges, from operations teams dealing with production issues, from product managers hearing customer needs, from upper management concerned about business objectives, and directly from customers themselves. All these voices inform your architectural decisions.

Determine Revised Requirements. You synthesize this feedback and identify what needs to change. Which concerns are most pressing? What opportunities exist to improve the system? What architectural shortcomings have become apparent? This synthesis transforms raw feedback into actionable architectural direction.

Update Architecture. You make necessary adjustments to your architectural vision. Sometimes these are small tweaks such as clarifying an interface, adjusting a pattern, or refining a guideline. Sometimes, when feedback reveals fundamental problems, you must make larger, more sweeping changes.

Facilitate Rollout of Changes. You work with all stakeholders to implement the updated architecture. This isn't just communicating new decisions. It's ensuring teams understand the reasoning, helping them integrate changes into their work, and providing support as they adapt to new approaches.

Then you return to gathering feedback, and the cycle continues. This constant loop of improvement keeps your architecture relevant as everything around it changes.

YOUR ROLE AS EVALUATOR

A major responsibility in managing churn is evaluating the constant stream of design proposals and architectural ideas that come from your teams. Every significant design initiative should pass through your review. This review serves multiple purposes.

You evaluate how the proposal fits into the overall architecture. Does it align with your architectural vision? Does it work with the patterns and approaches you've established? Or does it introduce unnecessary inconsistency?

You assess the impact on other components. How will this change affect other parts of the system? Will it require corresponding changes elsewhere? Does it create new dependencies or coupling that could cause problems later?

You consider technical debt implications. Does this proposal improve the application as a whole, reducing technical debt? Or does it take shortcuts that will create maintenance burden and complexity down the road?

You evaluate the broader context. Does this change move the application toward product and company goals? Is it good for customers? Does it improve performance, availability, or capabilities in meaningful ways?

Your evaluation must be direct and actionable. The developer who brings you a proposal needs clear guidance, not vague observations. Be specific about what works, what doesn't, and what needs to change.

BALANCING STABILITY AND CHANGE

Managing churn requires balancing two competing needs: the stability teams need to work effectively and the change necessary for the system to evolve.

Too much change creates chaos. Teams struggle to keep up with new patterns and approaches. Technical debt accumulates as half-implemented changes pile up. Productivity suffers as developers spend more time adapting to changes than building features.

Too little change creates stagnation. The architecture falls behind business needs. Technical debt still accumulates, but now from working around architectural limitations rather than from frequent changes. Eventually, the gap between what exists and what's needed becomes so large that major, disruptive rewrites become necessary.

Your job is finding the right pace of change It requires enough evolution to keep the architecture relevant, but not so much that teams can't absorb it.

EMBRACING CONTINUOUS EVOLUTION

Modern architecture isn't created in advance in isolation. It emerges through continuous collaboration and refinement. Your architectural vision today will, and should, differ from your vision six months from now. New information, new technologies, and new requirements will change what's optimal.

This doesn't mean you're constantly reversing decisions or creating instability. It means you're responsive to reality rather than rigidly attached to outdated plans. You maintain architectural principles while remaining flexible about specific implementations. You hold firm on what matters while adapting to new circumstances.

Part Five

The Architect Emerges

Chapter 14

♪ *The Coda* ♪

The hall was almost empty when Aaron arrived.

No musicians. No sound. Just the soft hum of air conditioning and the faint scent of old wood and brass.

Anton sat alone in the front row, his posture a little heavier than before, his baton resting across his knees like a relic.

Aaron hesitated at the aisle, suddenly aware of how different this visit felt.

Anton looked up and smiled. "Mr. Blake."

Aaron grinned. "You know, you can just call me Aaron."

Anton's smile deepened. "And yet, I suspect you've earned the title 'Mr.' now."

They sat together for a while, simply in silence.

After a bit, Aaron broke the silence, "You weren't at rehearsal this week."

Anton nodded slowly. "No. My hands have begun to shake. It's time I listen instead of lead."

Aaron frowned. "That sounds... final."

Anton looked at the empty stage. "Every conductor must one day set down the baton."

He glanced at Aaron. "I imagine you understand this now."

Aaron nodded quietly. "I do."

Anton chuckled softly. "You learned faster than I did."

"I had a good teacher."

"I merely reminded you to listen. The rest was already in you.

Anton leaned back, his eyes closing for a moment. "You see, Aaron, architecture and conducting are both acts of faith. You shape what you cannot control. You build patterns in chaos and trust that others will find meaning in them."

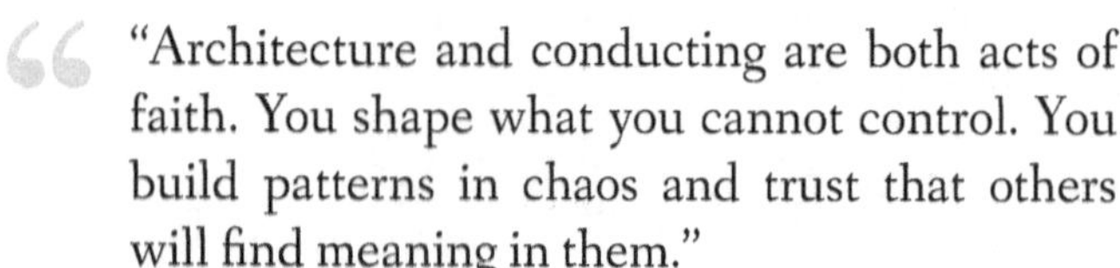

> "Architecture and conducting are both acts of faith. You shape what you cannot control. You build patterns in chaos and trust that others will find meaning in them."

He opened his eyes again. "And if you're lucky, sometimes they do."

Aaron studied him. The man who once commanded a hundred instruments with a flick of his wrist now sitting quietly among the echoes of past performances.

"Will you miss it?" he asked.

Anton smiled. "Absolutely. But silence is also part of the symphony."

He turned to Aaron. "And what will you do now?"

Aaron thought for a moment. "Keep learning. Keep listening. Maybe help others find their rhythm too."

Anton nodded. "Good. Then you are no longer my student."

Aaron smiled faintly. "Then what am I?"

Anton looked at him with a soft pride.

"A conductor."

The lights in the hall dimmed as the custodians began to close up.

Aaron stood. "Will you be all right?"

Anton nodded. "I have my music. You have yours."

He handed Aaron his baton. It was polished, worn smooth by decades of use.

"For when you forget what this feels like," Anton said. "It's lighter than it looks."

Aaron took it gently. "Marcus told me you called him. He says the rookie is ready."

Anton smiled. "He's right."

He looked at Aaron a long moment. "Goodbye... Mr. Blake."

Aaron left the hall. The rain had stopped, leaving the streets glazed in reflected light.

Aaron walked slowly toward the waterfront, the baton still in his hand.

He thought of Rachel and the way she saw empathy in design. He thought of Anton and the way he found order in sound. And he thought of himself. Of the way he once saw only code and now saw connection.

He smiled.

Architecture wasn't about control or complexity.

It was about *continuity*.

The baton passed on, the song unfinished, the rhythm still alive.

LESSON: THE ARCHITECT'S LEGACY

The architect's work is never finished. Only continued.

The best architectures, like the best symphonies, outlive their creators.

They evolve, adapt, and find new conductors. Each hears the music a little differently, each adds their own verse.

The architect's gift is not perfection. It's persistence.

To design in such a way that when you finally set down the baton, the music still plays.

Chapter 15

Interlude: Becoming a software architect

The transition from software developer to software architect is not a simple promotion. It represents a fundamental shift in how you work, what you're responsible for, and how you contribute to your organization. Understanding this transition, and the different paths that can lead you there, is essential for anyone considering this career move.

There are two primary paths into software architecture: growing into the role from within your current team or applying for an architectural position elsewhere. Both paths are valid. Both require different approaches. And both demand that you develop skills beyond what made you successful as a developer.

THE ORGANIC PATH: GROWING INTO ARCHITECTURE

Many architects don't apply for the role, they grow into it naturally as their responsibilities evolve. This organic transition often happens so gradually that you might not even realize you're becoming an architect until you're already doing the work.

This path typically begins when you're a senior developer who other team members start turning to for guidance. Junior developers ask you how the system works and how they should implement their changes. Your manager asks your advice on what's possible to implement. You find yourself spending more time on bigger-picture questions and less time on detailed, deep-dive coding.

You might notice you're being pulled into conversations about problems that impact the entire team or organization, not just your immediate area. You're thinking about scalability, availability, and operational concerns. These are issues that extend beyond any single component or feature. Management starts seeking your input on technical strategy and direction.

At some point, this informal architectural work starts conflicting with your coding responsibilities. You can't meet your development commitments because you're spending so much time helping others. This creates a decision point:

continue trying to do both jobs

or:

consciously shift your focus toward the architectural work.

When you talk to your manager about this tension, you might jointly decide to reduce your individual coding assignments and focus more on helping the rest of the team. This conscious decision to reprioritize represents the formal beginning of your transition into architecture, even if your job title doesn't change immediately.

This path of decreasing coding responsibilities while increasing focus on helping other developers become more productive, is common for senior developers moving into architecture. Eventually, you may leave the developer role entirely to focus full-time on the overall architecture of the product and enabling the rest of the team. As the product grows, this role becomes increasingly critical, and if you've demonstrated your ability to grow with those needs, you're perfectly positioned to move into a formalized architectural role when it becomes available.

The advantage of this path is that you already understand the product, the team, and the organization. You've built trust and credibility. The disadvantage is that it can be hard to fully transition to your new role. People may continue expecting you to write code and solve immediate problems even as your responsibilities shift.

THE APPLICATION PATH: SEEKING AN ARCHITECTURAL ROLE

The second path into architecture involves applying for an existing architectural position, either within your current company or at a new organization. This represents a more deliberate career change where you're actively seeking the role rather than growing into it organically.

This path often appeals to senior developers who are ready for new challenges but haven't had the opportunity to grow into an architectural role within their current team. Perhaps your team already has an architect. Perhaps the product is too small to justify a dedicated architectural role. Or perhaps you're simply ready for a change and see architecture as the next logical step in your career.

When you apply for an architectural position, you're making a conscious decision to leverage your development experience and product knowledge into a new type of role. You recognize that there's much to learn about the differences between being an architect and being a developer, but you believe your background and experience, combined with mentoring from peer architects and leadership, will enable you to take on the new responsibilities.

The advantage of this path is that you make a clean break of it. There is no ambiguity about your new role and responsibilities. You start with a fresh slate, building fresh relationships and establishing yourself as an architect from day one. The disadvantage is that you lack the organizational context and product knowledge that makes the organic path easier. You'll need to deliberately build those foundations while also learning your new role.

Even if a particular application doesn't work out, the decision to apply strengthens your resolve and clarifies your career direction. If not this specific role, there will be others. These may be in your company or elsewhere. But there are many architectural roles that you can pursue, and you can pursue them with increasing confidence and preparation.

UNDERSTANDING WHAT CHANGES

Before making the transition to architecture, whether organically or through application, you need to honestly assess whether this change aligns with what you want from your career. Sometimes the grass appears greener from the other side of the fence. It's easy to see the appealing aspects of a new role while underestimating the challenges or missing what you'll give up from your current position.

Ask yourself these questions:

Are you drawn to big-picture problems? Architecture focuses on broad, systemic challenges rather than detailed technical puzzles. If you love diving deep into specific technical problems and finding elegant solutions to focused challenges, you might find architecture frustrating.

Do you enjoy helping others solve problems more than solving them yourself? As an architect, your primary contribution shifts from direct implementation to enabling others to implement effectively. You'll spend less time writing production code and more time helping developers understand how to work within the system you're designing. This requires deriving satisfaction from others' success rather than your own direct accomplishments.

Can you make decisions with incomplete information? Architects make fewer but larger decisions, and they make them more slowly and with less certainty than developers typically experience. You won't have all the data you want. You'll need to balance competing priorities and accept that there's rarely one clearly correct answer. If you prefer situations with clear right answers and clear wrong answers, then architecture's ambiguity will be uncomfortable to you.

Do you want to work across organizational boundaries? Architects regularly coordinate with people outside the development organization, including product managers, business leaders, operations teams, and senior management. If you prefer to focus on technical work within a development team, you might find these interactions distracting. If you're energized by understanding different perspectives and translating between technical and non-technical stakeholders, this aspect of architecture could be fulfilling.

Are you ready to let go of being the hero? Many senior developers build their reputation and self-image around being the person who solves critical problems. Architecture requires you to shift from being the hero who fixes everything to being the coach who helps others develop their problem-solving capabilities. This transition can be emotionally challenging, even if intellectually you understand it's necessary.

Be honest with yourself about these questions. The transition from developer to architect is a significant change. You're not just taking on more responsibility or moving up a level. You are fundamentally changing the nature of your work.

TAKING PROACTIVE STEPS

If you're not yet an architect but want to become one, you can take specific actions to prepare for and accelerate this transition:

Take on additional responsibility beyond your immediate assignments. Look for opportunities to contribute to areas outside your direct responsibilities. Volunteer to help with cross-team coordination. Offer to document system architecture or integration patterns. These activities demonstrate broader thinking and begin developing the skills you'll need.

Identify and champion solutions to systemic problems. Look for problems that impact scalability, availability, or complexity. Find issues that affect operations but can be solved through technical changes. Focus on problems that have impact beyond your immediate area. When you identify these problems, don't just complain about them. Develop proposals for how to fix them. Managers respect people who bring solutions, not just problems.

Demonstrate architectural thinking in your current work. When you make technical decisions, explain your reasoning in terms of broader system impacts. Document not just what you did but why you made those choices and what alternatives you considered. Show that you're thinking about maintainability, scalability, and operational concerns, not just immediate functionality.

Build relationships across organizational boundaries. Start working with product managers, operations teams, and other stakeholders. Understand their concerns and constraints. Practice translating between technical and business language. These relationships will be crucial if you move into architecture and building them early demonstrates your readiness for the role.

Mentor others on your team. Start helping less experienced developers understand the system and make good technical decisions. This builds your teaching and coaching skills while demonstrating leadership. It also begins developing your potential successors, which makes it easier for your organization to support your transition.

WORKING WITH YOUR MANAGER

Whether you're growing organically into architecture or are actively seeking an architectural role, your manager is your most important ally in this transition. They can help guide you through the journey, identify opportunities for you to demonstrate architectural capabilities, and advocate for you when positions open up.

However, approaching this conversation requires care. Your manager may not warmly embrace the idea of you moving on, even if they think you'd make an excellent architect. If you're looking to transition, it's likely because you're one of the best developers on your team. Your manager may be reluctant to lose that capability.

Moving from developer to architect is different from moving from developer to senior developer or lead developer. Moving up the developer ladder means more responsibility and authority in the same domain. Moving to architecture means moving out of the developer role entirely. Your manager is losing a developer, and quite potentially their best developer. This can be hard for them to handle.

Be prepared for a difficult conversation. Even supportive managers may need convincing. The best approach is to talk about the bigger picture. Explain how your ability to take on a larger architectural role benefits the organization as a whole. But also, be understanding of their problem. They'll have a gap to fill.

Help your manager fill that gap. If you're a senior developer, you've probably already been mentoring junior developers. Talk to your manager about how other team members can grow into your current role. You should always, at all levels of responsibility, be working on developing your replacement. Your manager will be less hesitant to support your transition if you've done good work preparing someone to step into your shoes or made the team more self-supporting without you.

If your manager isn't supportive, don't give up. Your manager should be your first point of contact, but they don't have to be your last. Find allies. These can be other managers, senior developers, or other company leadership who can help. But don't undermine your manager in the process. Making your promotion a political issue will hurt you in the long run.

FINDING MENTORS

Throughout this transition, mentors become invaluable. A mentor who has already made the transition to architecture can help you navigate challenges, understand organizational dynamics, and develop the skills you need. They can speak to your manager as a peer, help you understand what it takes to succeed in your specific organizational context, and provide perspective when you're uncertain about decisions.

Your mentor might be inside your company or outside it. They might be a current architect in your organization, a senior leader who has seen many people make this transition, or someone you've met through professional networks or conferences. The key is finding someone who understands both the technical and organizational aspects of architecture and who is willing to invest in your development.

Don't wait until you're formally in an architectural role to seek a mentor. Start building these relationships while you're still a developer. The insights you gain will help you prepare for the transition and increase your chances of success when the opportunity arrives.

MAKING THE TRANSITION SUCCESSFULLY

Once you've moved into an architectural role, whether through organic growth or active application, specific actions will help you succeed in those critical early months:

Reach out to other architects. Find architects both inside and outside your organization who can help you get your feet wet. Learn from their experiences. Understand what worked for them and what challenges they faced. Build a peer network you can turn to for advice and perspective.

Connect with organizational leadership. Use your manager to build relationships with senior leaders. The best architects understand what's happening in their organizations and help find technical solutions to management's concerns. You need visibility into business strategy and priorities to make architectural decisions that truly serve the organization.

Understand business needs and requirements. Who drives business requirements in your organization? Why is your application important to the business? What problems is it solving? What competitive pressures exist? Architecture divorced from business context is just technical exercise.

Know the product deeply. Who manages the product? What do customers need? What's coming in the roadmap? Understanding product direction allows you to make architectural decisions that anticipate future needs rather than just solving immediate problems.

Get to know your developers. If you came from outside the development organization, learn about your team members. What are their strengths? What are their weaknesses? What skill gaps exist and what capabilities can you leverage? This understanding shapes everything from your architectural decisions to your communication approach.

Resist the urge to go back to your old role. If you came from the development organization you're now architecting for, you'll feel constant pressure to "fix" things yourself rather than helping others make things better. This temptation is natural. After all, you know you can solve the problem quickly. But giving in to this temptation undermines your new role and prevents others from developing their own capabilities.

THE EMOTIONAL JOURNEY

The transition from developer to architect is not just a change in responsibilities. It's an emotional journey that requires you to redefine how you derive satisfaction from your work.

As a developer, you get immediate feedback. You write code, see it work, feel the satisfaction of solving a specific problem. As an architect, satisfaction becomes more abstract and diffuse. You might spend weeks on decisions that won't show results for months. Your contributions become harder to point to because they're embedded in others' work.

You move from being the person who fixes problems to being the person who helps others develop the capability to fix problems. You shift from getting credit for your solutions to enabling others to create solutions. This requires finding fulfillment in others' success rather than your own visible accomplishments.

You also lose some of the clear boundaries that make development work satisfying. As a developer, you can close your laptop at the end of the day knowing you've completed specific tasks. As an architect, work becomes less bounded. There's always another concern to consider, another stakeholder to coordinate with, another decision to make. Learning to manage this unbounded nature of architectural work is part of the transition.

The transition can feel isolating. You're no longer fully part of the development team. You've moved to a different role with different concerns. Yet, you're not quite management either. You occupy a middle space that can feel lonely, especially in the early months before you've built relationships with other architects and found your footing in the new role.

These emotional aspects of the transition are real and valid. Acknowledging them rather than dismissing them helps you navigate them successfully. Find peers, such as other architects, mentors, or leaders, who understand what you're experiencing. Their perspective and support will make the journey easier.

KNOWING IF THIS IS RIGHT FOR YOU

Not everyone should become an architect. Being a senior developer is an important, valuable, and fulfilling career. Moving into architecture isn't the only path forward, and it isn't inherently better than remaining a developer.

Architecture is right for you if:

- You're energized by big-picture thinking and systemic problems. You enjoy understanding how pieces fit together more than diving deep into any single piece. You want to influence the direction of entire systems and organizations, not just individual components.
- You derive satisfaction from others' success. You get more fulfillment from helping a developer solve a problem than from solving it yourself. You want to multiply your impact by enabling others rather than maximizing your individual contribution.
- You're comfortable with ambiguity and uncertainty. You can make decisions with incomplete information and live with the knowledge that you might be wrong. You

understand that architectural decisions involve tradeoffs with no clearly correct answer.
- You want to work across organizational boundaries. You're interested in business context, product strategy, and organizational dynamics. You want to translate between technical and non-technical stakeholders and help align technical decisions with business needs.

Architecture might not be right for you if you love the craft of coding itself, prefer clear problems with definite solutions, want to see immediate results from your work, or prefer to stay within technical domains rather than engaging with broader organizational concerns. These preferences don't make you less valuable. In fact, they may make you more valuable. But what they do is they make you a different type of contributor. Organizations need both developers and architects to succeed.

TAKING THE LEAP

Whether you're growing organically into architecture or actively pursuing an architectural role, this transition represents an exciting and challenging time in your career. You're moving into new territory with new responsibilities and new opportunities to make an impact.

The transition will be difficult. You'll face moments of uncertainty about whether you made the right choice. You'll struggle with letting go of the familiar comforts of development work. You'll make mistakes as you learn what effective architecture looks like in practice rather than theory.

But if architecture aligns with your interests and strengths, this transition opens up possibilities that weren't available as a developer. You gain influence over system-wide decisions. You shape how entire teams work and what they build. You develop skills in leadership, communication, and strategic thinking that expand your career options for the rest of your professional life.

The transition from developer to architect is significant. But with clear understanding of what you're moving toward, deliberate preparation for the skills you'll need, and patience with yourself as you learn, you can make this transition successfully and build a fulfilling career in software architecture.

♪ Epilogue ♪

Months later, Aaron visited the concert hall again. The stage was empty, the seats dark.

He sat in the center row, baton in hand, notebook open.

In the margin of his notes, he wrote:

> *"To design is to conduct. To build is to perform. To understand both, that is architecture."*

He closed the notebook, smiled to himself, and whispered into the quiet:

"Your turn."

♪ ♪ ♪

The next morning, Aaron was at work in his office, the chief architect for the company. Others depended on him now, as he depended on them. He needed them to perform, while he conducted.

A promising young developer knocked at his door.

"Sir. I need help."

Aaron responded, "What's up?"

"Well sir," the young developer stammered, "I have this great idea for how to rewrite the job queuing system, but I can't get anyone to listen to me."

Aaron smiled. "Why is that?"

"Well, I don't know. I know it's a great idea, but how can you convince other people to listen to your ideas? You do it all the time, how can I do it?"

Aaron's smile broadened. "Do you have plans tonight?"

"No, I, I, I don't," the younger developer said. "Wha... Why?"

"We're going to an orchestra concert."

Author's Reflections

Aaron's story isn't unique.

In fact, it's one I've seen many times. I've lived through it myself.

Every developer who begins to sense "there's something more" faces the same moment Aaron did: that quiet dissatisfaction when coding no longer feels like creating, when success isn't just about making things work, but about understanding *why they work at all.*

That's the moment you start thinking like an architect.

Becoming a software architect isn't a promotion. It's a perspective shift.

You stop measuring your value by how much code you write and start measuring it by how well others can build around you. You learn to see systems as living things. Systems are full of dependencies, constraints, and people.

And just like an orchestra, those systems need more than technical excellence.

They need harmony.

When Anton told Aaron, *"You must listen before you lead,"* he wasn't just teaching him how to conduct. He was describing the essence of architectural thinking.

Architects listen for imbalance. Imbalance in design, in process, in communication. They translate chaos into coherence. They build clarity where there was confusion.

But they don't do it alone.

The best architectures, and the best teams, happen when empathy meets structure.

When vision meets humility.

When logic meets listening.

That's the balance Aaron learned from Rachel and Anton. It's the same balance every great architect learns over time.

If you are early in your journey, don't rush to grab the baton. Start by listening. Understand the rhythms of your team, the themes of your system, the tone of your company's goals.

Then, when the time comes to lead, don't try to play every instrument. Help others play beautifully together. Because that's what architecture really is.

It's not control. It's not authority. It's *composition*.

You're not building software. You are writing a symphony of collaboration, resilience, and purpose.

And one day, someone else will pick up where you left off, and the music will continue.

Lee Atchison
Architect, Conductor, Author
Seattle, Washington
leeatchison.com

About the Author

Lee Atchison is a CTO, Chief Software Architect, author, and thought leader. Lee is the author of multiple books, including the O'Reilly Media titles *Architecting for Scale* and *Overcoming IT Complexity*. He is the co-author of *Business Breakthrough 3.0*.

Lee has developed numerous courses for *O'Reilly Media*, *LinkedIn Learning*, *Coursera*, and other learning platforms. Lee writes articles regularly and has been a featured writer at *InfoWorld* and at *Cloud Native Now* (*formerly Container Journal*). Lee is a guest co-host on the highly popular technology podcast *Software Engineering Daily*. Lee is the host of his own successful newsletter and podcast *Software Architecture Insights*.

Lee has written e-books as a thought leader for companies including *Redis*, *Uptycs*, and *F5*, and has consulted with larger companies including *Bank of America*, *OutSystems*, *Seagate*, and smaller companies, such as *Ory*, *Netdata*, *CAST Software*, and *Blameless*. Lee has shared his expertise with companies from Nike, to Deutsche Telecom, to Starbucks, to Walt Disney Company, to Major League Baseball.

Lee produces content that is focused on modern applications, cloud-based applications, availability, scaling, DevOps, AI/ML, IT security, and other related topics.

Lee has been CTO, Chief Architect, and Software Engineering Director at many companies, including Amazon.com, AWS, New Relic, Blameless, and Hewlett Packard. Lee was a co-founder of the AI-focused startup company, Product Genius.

Lee is available for writing, speaking, and consulting.

♪ ♪ ♪

Over the course of my nearly forty year career in software engineering, there have been many people who have influenced me and driven my experiences that ultimately led to this book. There are just too many to mention them all, and of course I risk forgetting to name important ones.

So, instead, I just want to mention the one person that has brought it all into focus. The one person who has kept me happy. Fulfilled. Loved. Adored. Cherished. The one person who means everything to me. My lovely wife Beth. Without her, none of this would have been possible.

linkedin.com/in/leeatchison

amazon.com/author/leeatchison

instagram.com/leeatchison